AF375480

Dedicated to Our Khon (Child), Soma Khim Turner Hong.

Puk says, "Chom reap sour".
Mami says, "Hola".
That means hello!
TAXI

Puk says,
"Leahaey".
Mami says:
"Adios".
That means
goodbye!

Puk says,
"Arun sour sdey".

Mami says,
"Buenos dias".

That means
good morning!

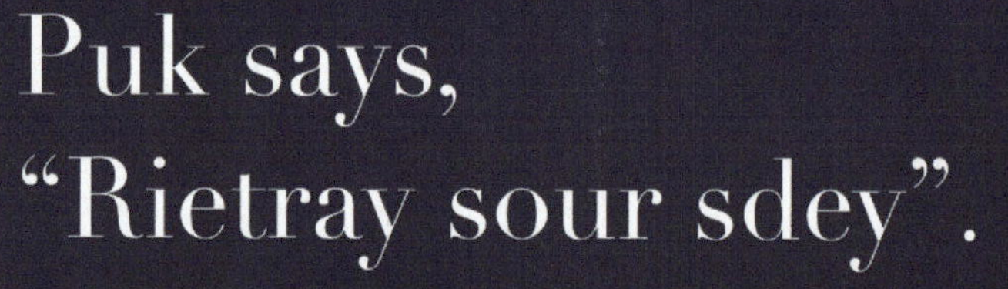

That means
good night!

Puk says,
"Som thaeb muy".

Mami says,
"Dame un
beso".

That means
give me a kiss!

Puk says,
"Bong srolanh oun".

Mami says,
"Te amo".

That means
I love you!

Mami says,
"Como estas"?

Puk says,
"Sok sabai"?

That means
how are you?

Puk says,
"Somnang la-arh".
Mami says,
"Buena suerte
That means
good luck!

Mami says,
"Muchas
gracias".
'uk says,
Aurkhun chroeun".
That means
thank you
so much!

Puk says,
"Ayou weinh".

Mami says,
"Que tengas un
larga vida".

That means
live a long life

Thank you to the following people for the support in the process of making this book: Tamara Turner, Hilda Milian and B. Ruiz.

MTA
New York City
Subway